All Quiet on the Western Front

Erich Remarque

TEACHER GUIDE

NOTE:

The trade book edition of the novel used to prepare this guide is found in the Novel Units catalog and on the Novel Units website. Using other editions may have varied page references.

Please note: We have assigned Interest Levels based on our knowledge of the themes and ideas of the books included in the Novel Units sets, however, please assess the appropriateness of this novel or trade book for the age level and maturity of your students prior to reading with them. You know your students best!

ISBN 978-1-56137-619-3

Copyright infringement is a violation of Federal Law.

© 2020 by Novel Units, Inc., St. Louis, MO. All rights reserved. No part of this publication may be reproduced, translated, stored in a retrieval system, or transmitted in any way or by any means (electronic, mechanical, photocopying, recording, or otherwise) without prior written permission from Novel Units, Inc.

Reproduction of any part of this publication for an entire school or for a school system, by for-profit institutions and tutoring centers, or for commercial sale is strictly prohibited.

Novel Units is a registered trademark of Conn Education.

Printed in the United States of America.

To order, contact your local school supply store, or:

Toll-Free Fax: 877.716.7272
Phone: 888.650.4224
3901 Union Blvd., Suite 155
St. Louis, MO 63115

sales@novelunits.com

novelunits.com

Table of Contents

Plot Summary 3

Background Information: World War I...4

Background on the Novelist 5

Initiating Activities...5

Vocabulary, Discussion Questions,
Writing Ideas, Activities
    Chapters 1-2 8
        Literary Analysis: Setting..10
    Chapters 3-4 10
        Literary Analysis: Theme...12
    Chapter 5 12
        Literary Analysis: Imagery...14
    Chapter 6 14
        Literary Analysis: Contrast..16
    Chapter 7 16
        Literary Analysis: Irony...18
    Chapters 8-9 18
        Literary Analysis: Point of View..20
    Chapter 10 21
        Literary Analysis: Satire..22
    Chapters 11-12 22
        Literary Analysis: Symbol..24

Post-Reading Extension Activities 25
    Questions for Discussion or Writing 25
    Suggested Further Reading..26
    Writing 26
    Listening/Speaking 27
    Drama 28
    Art 28
    Music 28
    Research 28

Plot Summary

Paul, a 19-year-old German soldier describes his experiences during World War I as they unfold. As the story begins, Paul's friend Josef Behm has already been killed. During a recent attack the English killed nearly half of the company, and as a result the survivors are enjoying extra food and cigarettes. Most of the friends Paul sketches in the first chapter die later: Müller, who still carries his textbooks; Leer, who enjoys visiting the officer's brothel; Tjaden, a skinny locksmith; Albert Kropp, clear-thinker; Haie Westhus, a hearty peat-digger; Detering, a peasant who misses his farm; Katczinsky, the resourceful 40-year-old leader of the group; Kemmerich, who is at St. Joseph's with a thigh wound.

A letter has come from the friends' former schoolmaster, Kantorek, who had urged his students to enlist. As the group reminisces about Kantorek, Paul reflects on how men like him glorify war and send off the young to fight and die. When Paul and the others visit Kemmerich, whose leg has been amputated, it is clear that he is dying. Müller asks for his boots, but Kemmerich refuses. Later, as Kemmerich weeps, Paul thinks of having to tell Kemmerich's mother. Kemmerich dies, and Paul takes his boots to Müller.

Within three weeks of joining the army, Paul and the others discovered how demeaning the training regimen is—and how abusive their superiors can be. The friends particularly dislike Himmelstoss, a former postmaster who is now a corporal and who took a dislike to Paul and his friends during training. One night they waited to ambush him with a bedsheet, covered him so that he could not see his attackers, and got their revenge by whipping him.

Paul and the others were sent to the front and discovered weeks later that Himmelstoss is arriving at the front, too. Now that he is expected to fight side by side with these men, he tries to befriend them, but Tjaden, Kropp and the others remember past injustices and rebuff him with insults. The unit, which has been given the assignment to put up barbed wire, is bombarded. The men escape into a cemetery, with coffins bursting open around them. Several wounded horses scream in pain. A young recruit is badly injured and Kat and Paul consider shooting him to end his misery. Kat manages to kill a goose while Paul fends off a dog, and the two share a feast with Kropp and Tjaden.

The unit is sent to the front and there is a bloody offensive. Hungry and demoralized, the unit lies in the trenches; one young recruit has a fit; Paul and Kat beat him to prevent him from running out from cover. Paul has disquieting memories of peaceful times, but realizes that "quietness [is] unobtainable for us now." Someone cries in pain for days, but the others cannot find him. Paul finds Himmelstoss cowering in a dug-out and orders him to fight. Haie Westhus is mortally wounded in the back; only 32 men from the Second Company remain alive.

Now that summer is past, the unit is sent to the rear to rest. Paul, Leer, and Kropp arrange a rendezvous with some young women. When Paul goes home on a 17-day leave, he is depressed to find that his mother's health is failing—and that he himself has changed. He no longer belongs at home; his dreams for the future have been shattered.

Paul is sent to a training camp adjoining a Russian prison camp. He finds it strange to see the enemy so close—and to realize that they are men much like himself, enemies only because a word of command has been issued.

Paul returns to his unit in time for an inspection by the Kaiser. In a climactic scene, Paul kills a French soldier who jumps into a shell-hole where Paul has been hiding. It takes a while for the soldier to die, and Paul is conscience-stricken. At first he promises himself that he will personally notify the man's family, but realizes later that he will not.

Eight members of Paul's unit are given a comparatively good job—guarding an abandoned village. At one point they prepare a grand feed, with Paul frying pancakes while dodging shells. Later Kropp and Paul are both wounded; Kropp says that he will kill himself if he loses his leg. The two are sent to the hospital together. Albert's leg is amputated and Paul is operated on. The wife of one of the other wounded soldiers comes for a visit and Albert plays with the baby while the husband and wife make love.

One by one, Paul's classmates are killed in the most bloody summer of the war, the summer of 1918. Armistice is near at hand but it is too late for Paul's friends—including his best friend, Kat, who is killed by a flying splinter while Paul attempts to carry him to safety. Fall arrives and finds Paul assigned two weeks of rest after swallowing some gas. Paul feels alone, without hope and also without fear.

On the last page, narration switches to the third person and the reader learns that Paul, too, has died. "He fell in October 1918...his face had an expression of calm, as though almost glad the end had come."

Background Information:
World War I

WWI (1914-18), often called the Great War, was a conflict of tremendous size and destructiveness. Modern devices of war such as poison gas, machine guns and aircraft were first used on a large scale. Territorial conflicts came to a head when Austrian Archduke Ferdinand was assassinated by a Serbian nationalist in 1914. By the end of 1915 the Central Powers (Austria-Hungary, Germany, Bulgaria, the Ottoman Empire) were fighting the Allies (Great Britain, Russia, Italy, France, Belgium, Serbia, Montenegro, Japan and—following the sinking of the Lusitania in 1917—the U.S.). The war took a ghastly toll: at least 13 million military deaths and twice that number of wounded. Over 9 million civilians died and over 400 billion dollars were spent on the war effort.

Background Information:
Erich Maria Remarque

Born in Osnabruck, Germany, in 1898, Remarque was wounded five times during combat in World War I. Afterward, he worked as a teacher, a stonecutter, and an assistant editor. Then he attained wealth and international fame with publication of his war novel, *All Quiet on the Western Front.* Successful as it was, some German critics assailed the novel for promoting pacifism and others leveled the opposite charge—that the book was a piece of romantic propaganda for war.

Most of his subsequent nine novels also depict the destruction of youth by war. *The Road Back* describes how difficult it is for the veteran to reintegrate into the civilian world. *Three Comrades* is about three veterans who struggle to readjust in politically ravaged post-war Germany. *Flotsam* and *Arch of Triumph* chronicle the pitiable fate of refugees from Hitler's Germany. *The Black Obelisk* is set during the inflation years after World War I. *Heaven Has No Favorites* is about a girl with TB who falls in love with a race car driver.

In 1929 Remarque moved to Switzerland. When he persisted in criticizing the Nazi party, his books were burned and his movies were banned in Germany. He visited the U.S. in 1939 and moved there eight years later. Although he had become an American citizen, he moved back to Switzerland after World War II. He died in 1970 at age 72.

Initiating Activities

Choose one or more of the following activities to establish an appropriate mind set for the story students are about to read:

1. **Anticipation Guide** (See *Novel Units Student Packet,* Activity #1): Students discuss their opinions of statements which tap themes they will meet in the story. For example:
    a)   Suffering builds a man's character.
    b)   It is wrong to kill another human being.
    c)   Any war could have been prevented.
    d)   Power corrupts.
    e)   Revenge is sweet.

2. **Video:** Two film versions of the novel were made: the Academy Award winning black and white version with Lew Ayres (directed by Lewis Milestone, 1930) and the more recent color version (directed by Delbert Mann, 1979) with Ernest Borgnine.

3. **Research:** Have students research the background of World War I (see Background Information, page 2). You might show a film such as "Causes of World War I," a scholarly program that combines documentary visuals with narrative (color, 35 minutes, EAV).

4. **Log:** Have students keep a response log as they read.

   a) In one type of log, the student assumes the persona of one of the characters. Writing on one side of each piece of paper, the student writes in the first person ("I...") about his or her reactions to one episode in that chapter. A partner (or the teacher) responds to these writings on the other side of the paper, as if talking to the character.

   b) In the dual entry log, students jot down brief summaries and reactions to each section of the novel they have read. The first entry could be made based on a preview of the novel—a glance at the cover and a flip through the book.

Pages	Summary	Reactions
		These might begin: "I liked the part where...," "This reminded me of the time I...," "Paul reminds me of another character...," "If I were Paul I wouldn't..."

5. **Verbal Scales:** Choose one or more of the following scales. After students finish a section of the story, have them chart Paul's feelings and judgments about the war using the scales you selected. After each section, ask "How does Paul feel about the war?" Students should discuss their ratings, using evidence from the story.

Patriotic	0 • 1 • 2 • 3 • 4 • 5
Devoted to Principle	0 • 1 • 2 • 3 • 4 • 5
Hopeful	0 • 1 • 2 • 3 • 4 • 5
Homesick	0 • 1 • 2 • 3 • 4 • 5
Despairing	0 • 1 • 2 • 3 • 4 • 5
Depressed	0 • 1 • 2 • 3 • 4 • 5
Compliant	0 • 1 • 2 • 3 • 4 • 5
Defiant	0 • 1 • 2 • 3 • 4 • 5

To help students become aware of the way Remarque alternates violent scenes with more peaceful ones, you might ask students to rate the atmosphere of each chapter on the following scale:

peaceful/relaxed   **1 2 3 4 5 6 7**   *violent*

6. **Brainstorming:** Have students generate associations with a theme that is central to the story while a student scribe jots ideas around the central word or statement on a large piece of paper. Help students "cluster" the ideas into categories. A sample framework is shown below.

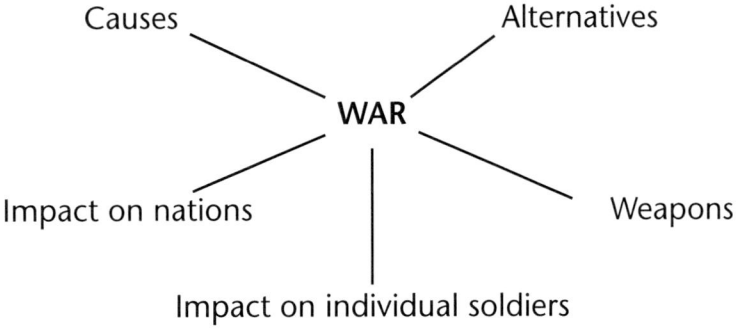

7. **Geography:** Have students examine a map of Germany. Have them locate the "Western Front" (area facing France) and the "Eastern Front" (facing what was then Russia).

8. **Prediction:** After students have glanced at the title, cover picture and blurbs, ask: What sort of story is this? What is happening in the picture? How are the two young men feeling? What is the "Western Front"? (During World War I, German soldiers fought on the Eastern front—the side facing Russia—and the Western front—the side facing France, the area where the more bloody conflicts occurred.) Ask: When do you think it is "all quiet" on the Western Front?

Vocabulary • Discussion Questions
Writing Ideas • Activities

Chapters 1-2

Vocabulary

dollop 1	voracity 1	quids 2	windfall 2
queue 3	disconcerted 4	dust-up 6	dixie 6
billets 7	latrine 7	pithily 8	martinets 11
ostracized 11	mediators 12	mutineers 13	rails 18
renunciation 22	disciplinarian 23	discomfiture 24	saveloy 33

Vocabulary Activity

Word mapping is an activity that lends itself to any vocabulary list. For words that have no antonyms, students provide a picture or symbol that captures the word meaning.

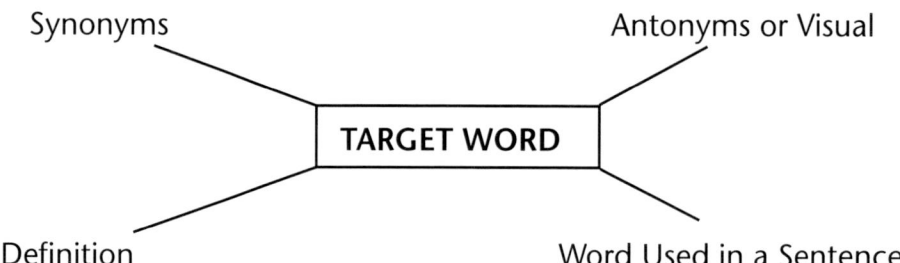

Discussion Questions

1. What do you "see" in your mind's eye as the story opens? What do you hear? smell? taste? (Answers should reflect the fact that the story opens on an army camp where the red-haired cook has been serving soldiers extra rations of sausage and bread.)

2. What is your impression of Paul Baumer? What information do you have to go on? (the 19-year-old narrator's own comments; He seems to be a good observer, has a sense of humor.) What do you suppose he looks like? Would he be a friend of yours?

Draw the following attribute web on the board; have students suggest Paul's characteristics and locate supportive evidence in the text as you jot these down on the board.

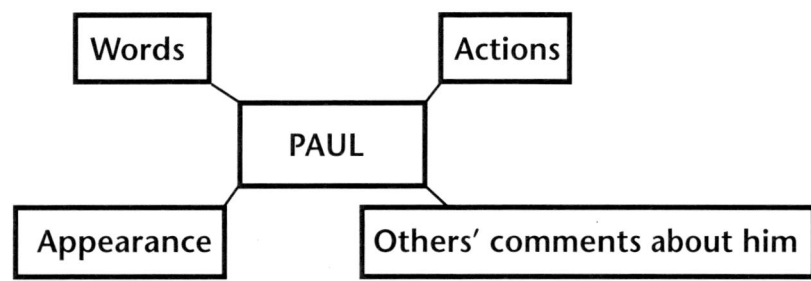

3. How can you tell that the recruits have had to give up much of their modesty and need for privacy? [They use a general latrine; "Since then we have learned better than to be shy about such trifling immodesties." page 8)] Have you ever had a similar experience?

4. What pleasures do Paul and the others have? (They enjoy chatting at the latrine, playing cards.) How worried do they seem to be about the possibility of dying? (They choose to ignore it when they can.)

5. What does Paul mean when he says, "It is very queer that the unhappiness of the world is so often brought on by small men" (page 10)? What does this have to do with Kantorek? (Authority figures like the teacher, Kantorek, start and promote the war while young men fight it.) Do you agree with that generalization?

6. Who was Behm? (a former classmate of Paul's; one of the first killed) Paul says that Behm hesitated about joining the war effort. Why didn't he refuse to join up, then? What was the result? (Kantorek urged him to join up; by volunteering, he died before the time he would have been forced to enlist.)

7. In what ways does Paul feel that the adults have let the young men down? (The younger ones trusted the older ones to guide them into the future; instead the older men ambushed their future by convincing them that it was their duty to go to war.) Do you think he is blaming them unfairly?

8. If you were filming the scene where Paul and the others visit Kemmerich, what would you show? What emotions would you emphasize? Where would you use close-ups?

9. According to Paul, how is war different for younger soldiers than it is for older ones? Do you think that is true? (Older ones have families, jobs to return to; younger men know nothing but war.)

10. How have the young men's attitudes toward war changed? (They see that it is deadly, not glorious.) What does Paul mean, "We learned that a bright button is weightier than four volumes of Schopenhauer" (page 21)? (They were evaluated on petty things like how shiny their buttons were, not their academic knowledge; Schopenhauer was a German philosopher who cited compassion as the foundation of ethics.) Does that change in attitude remind you of any other war stories you have seen or read? (e.g., *The Red Badge of Courage*)

11. What words and phrases might you use to describe Himmelstoss? (pompous, sadistic, strict, self-important, authoritarian) Do you think Himmelstoss is sadistic—or is he giving his men good preparation for the dangers they will meet? What does Paul think of him? (Paul hates him.) Have you ever known anyone like him?

12. Does Kemmerich know that he is dying? (When Paul mentions surviving the operation, Kemmerich says, "I don't think so.") Does Paul know? (Paul recognizes the signs of death coming on.) Do you think Paul does the right thing when he cuts off Kemmerich's talk of death by saying, "Don't talk rubbish"? Why is Paul angry with the doctor? (The doctor rationalizes his inattention to Kemmerich by pointing out that Kemmerich is only one of many amputations and deaths that day.) Is Paul right to be angry?

    PREDICTION: How many of Paul's friends introduced in Chapter One will be alive at the end of the novel?

Writing Ideas

a. Kropp gets angry when he learns what is in the letter from his former teacher, Kantorek. Suppose Kropp decides to write a letter to Kantorek telling how he really feels about the war—and about Kantorek's attitude toward the young soldiers. Write the letter.

b. Write the letter that Paul sends to Kemmerich's mother.

Literary Analysis: Setting
The setting is the time and place of events in the story. Discuss the setting of this novel. (behind the German front lines during the second half of World War I) Elicit students' impressions of what it would have been like to be a soldier at the front.

Chapters 3-4

Vocabulary

patronizingly 36	canteen 38	decorum 44	sallow 46
indefatigable 49	lorries 51	aspirants 52	acrid 52
bombardment 53	indigent 56	fete 60	baseness 64
restive 65			

Discussion Questions

1. How do Kat, Paul and the others treat the reinforcements? (They stick out their chests, tease them, try to help them "learn the ropes.") Do you think this is typical of how newer recruits are treated by more seasoned soldiers today?

2. How do the soldiers demonstrate camaraderie? (Kat shares food and supplies he finds; they enjoy talking with each other.)

3. What does Kat mean by his rhyme, "Give 'em all the same grub and all the same pay/And the war would be over and done in a day"? (page 41) (Kat reasons that if those in power had to experience what those in the field did, they wouldn't be willing to engage in as many wars.) Do you agree? Is Kat unpatriotic?

4. What does Kropp mean when he says that "As sure as [men like Himmelstoss] get a stripe or a star they become different men, just as though they'd swallowed concrete"? (Give people a little power and it goes to their heads.) Do you think that this is true in the U.S. military today? In any other occupations?

5. Why does Tjaden have a special grudge against Himmelstoss? (Himmelstoss punished him for bedwetting by making him sleep in a bunk below another bedwetter.) What could Tjaden have done when Himmelstoss treated him this way? (reported him) How does Tjaden ultimately get his revenge?

6. In what tone of voice do you imagine Paul saying, "Himmelstoss ought to have been pleased...We had become successful students of his method" (page 49)? (ironic) Do you think that Paul and the others reduce themselves to Himmelstoss's level by beating him? Aren't they being bullies now?

7. What is meant by the comparison between the camouflaged gun emplacements and "a kind of military Feast of the Tabernacles" (page 52)? (The cheerful bushes over the emplacements are reminiscent of the skin-covered tent supposedly constructed under instructions from God—and used by the Jews as a worship place—wherein the Ark of the Covenant was hidden by a veil.)

8. How does Paul feel as he reaches the front? How do he and the others "become on the instant human animals" (page 56)? (Their actions become automatic, instinctive efforts to survive.)

9. How does Paul respond when he sees that the young recruit is terrified? (He reassures the recruit, puts the helmet on his behind.) What thoughts cross his mind? (As the young soldier hugs him, Paul thinks of Kemmerich and feels sorry for the soldier who is so young.) What does this show you about Paul? (He is compassionate.) What happens to the young recruit in the end? (He is wounded and will die.) What do you think of Paul's agreeing with Kat to "put him out of his misery"? Why don't they go ahead and do it? (Others come.)

10. Why does the screaming of the horses bother Detering so much? (Detering was a farmer in civilian life.) Are you surprised that he is so upset by the suffering of the animals—when people are dying all around him?

11. Does Paul owe Kat his life? What do you think would have happened if Kat hadn't warned him about the gas? (Paul might have failed to put on his mask.) How is warfare similar today to what Paul experienced? How is it different?

12. What happens in the cemetery? (Kat's unit takes refuge from shelling there.) How do Kat and the others use the coffins? (They use some of the planks to help set wounded limbs.) Do you see any irony here?

    PREDICTION: What will happen when Paul and his friends encounter Himmelstoss at the front? How will they treat him?

Writing Idea: Kat is extremely resourceful. He has a knack for finding food, supplies—whatever he and his friends need. Does he remind you of anyone you know? Describe the most resourceful person you know.

Literary Analysis: Theme
A **theme** is one of the central ideas of a literary work. Clues to theme include: the title, what characters learn, direct comments by the characters or narrator, repeated phrases. How does Remarque develop the theme of the soldier's relationship to the earth? What is he saying about that relationship? (Paul comments, "When [the soldier] presses himself down upon [the earth] long and powerfully, when he buries his face and his limbs deep in her from the fear of death by shell-fire, then she is his only friend, his brother, his mother..."—page 55.) Later, Paul and the others take refuge in the cemetery, lying in the dirt with corpses. While the earth sustains life, it can swallow life in a moment. Soldiers are perpetually within a hair's breadth of death—of "returning to the earth."

Chapter 5

Vocabulary

levies 77	insatiable 77	laconically 78	dram 79
inquisitor 80	disconcerted 82	pince-nez 85	pensiveness 86
possy 89	conjectures 90	skat 91	communion 94
gusto 96			

Discussion Questions

1. Why do you think the author includes such a mundane detail as the killing of lice? If you were filming this story, would you include that scene? Why or why not?

2. How do the recruits feel about Himmelstoss's impending arrival? (They are satisfied by the news, probably because they are happy that he, whom they despise, will now have to risk his life.) Do you think Himmelstoss is aware of how the men feel? Do you think he cares? (He is angry when they act hostile.)

3. Why do you think Müller enjoys asking everyone what they would do if it were peacetime? Does everyone enjoy speculating about that? (Kropp is irritated by the question at first.) Why is everyone surprised by Haie Westhus' answer? (He says that he would stay in the peacetime military.) How do you explain the way he feels? (He is depressed by the thought of returning to a life of peat-digging.)

4. The narrator tells us that Himmelstoss "has already had some rot dinned into him about getting a shot in the back" (page 82). What does that mean? (Others have warned him about hated officers whose own men have shot them.)

5. How can you tell that Himmelstoss has lost much of the control he once had over the men? Why has he lost it? (Tjaden refuses his order to stand; the men are no longer in training under him, but at the dangerous front.)

6. Throughout the novel, the narrator refers to the fact that the war is harder on young men than on older ones. Where do you see that theme treated in this chapter? (Paul, Albert and the others talk about the "common fate of our generation"—that the war has interrupted young mens' lives just as they begin striving for success.)

7. Why do you think the young men spent so much time planning to get back at Himmelstoss? In what tone do you imagine Paul commenting, "That is our sole ambition: to knock the conceit out of a postman." (sarcastic, perhaps) Is he ashamed? (He sees how absurd it is to obsess about humiliating the petty Himmelstoss.)

8. Why is Tjaden on trial? (Himmelstoss reported him for refusing an order.) Why doesn't he get in more trouble than he does? (The lieutenant is sympathetic.) Do you think Tjaden deserved his punishment? Why does Kropp get one day's open arrest? (He doesn't go rushing to look for Tjaden, as Himmelstoss would like, and talks back to Himmelstoss.) What do you think would have happened if Tjaden or Kropp had acted as they did toward a supervisor in the workplace?

9. What do you imagine as you read the description of how Paul and Kat obtain the goose? Who do you suppose owns the goose? Why don't the soldiers just ask for the goose, or offer to buy it? (They were accustomed to taking what they could find.)

10. How do Paul and Kat feel as they eat the goose? (contented, satisfied, a sense of communion with each other) Have you ever felt such a sense of communion with someone else?

11. Why do you think Paul likes Kat so much? (Kat is direct, resourceful, mature, kind.) Would they have been friends during peacetime?

12. What is the tone of the final sentence of the chapter: "The outlines of the huts are upon us in the dawn like a dark, deep sleep"? (tranquil tone; grim contentment) How content or agitated does Paul seem at this point in the story?

    PREDICTION: Haie Westhus is the only one of the group who says that he would stay in the military during peace time. Do you think any of the others will change their minds later?

Writing Idea
Suppose that you are a young cousin of Paul's. You receive a post-card from Paul. Design the post-card with an illustration of a scene from the story on one side. Design a stamp that shows something of the story's setting. Write a brief sentence about the scene in the space where such a description usually appears on a postcard (left-hand corner). Write the message. Don't forget the postmark (time/place). Separate the message from the address by writing the title and author vertically between the two.

Literary Analysis: Imagery
Imagery means the use of details that appeal to the senses of sight, hearing, taste, smell, and touch. Reread the section describing how Kat and Paul catch and cook the goose (pages 92-97). Consider how the passage helps readers imagine that they can see, hear, taste, and feel what is being described. List images that appeal to each of the senses (sight, hearing, smell, taste, touch). What feelings are conveyed by the description?

Chapter 6

Vocabulary

offensive 99	surpasses 100	unscathed 101	repulsive 102
spades 104	parapet 106	convulsion 106	disabuse 107
glowering 109	claustrophobia 109	impinges 114	automata 115
debauched 115	stupor 115	cowers 116	provisions 118
benediction 118	cloister 119	apparitions 120	allurement 120
inapprehensible 121	solace 123	trenches 124	scrutinize 125
chloroform 126	putrefaction 126	equanimity 127	shrapnel 128
reinforcements 129	hemorrhages 131	cur 132	barrage 132
docile 134	pallid 135		

Discussion Questions
1. What do you "see" as the soldiers march to the front? Why do they joke about the rows of coffins? (They realize that the coffins are meant for them.)
2. Why are Paul and the others in low spirits? How have they been affected by "friendly fire"? (German shells are falling in the trenches, wounding German soldiers, because the barrels are worn out.) Is "friendly fire" still a problem in modern warfare? (yes)

3. Why does Paul say that "the front is a cage"? (page 101) (The soldiers feel trapped, waiting helplessly for whatever happens.) Why does Paul believe in Chance? (Many times he was saved when he might have been hit.) Do you?

4. How—and why—do the men "make war on the rats"? (The rats are gnawing on the men's food, so the soldiers hunt the rats by putting bait in the center of the room and waiting with flashlights.)

5. What causes the young recruit to begin to "crack"? What chain of events does this set in motion?

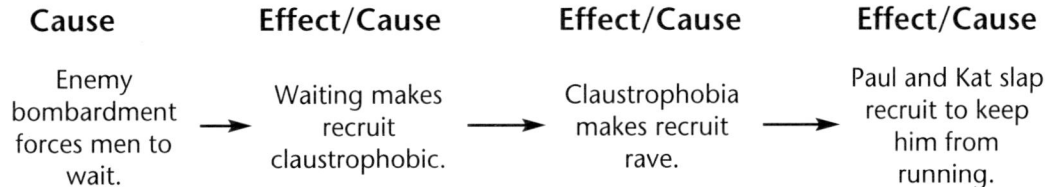

Cause	Effect/Cause	Effect/Cause	Effect/Cause
Enemy bombardment forces men to wait.	Waiting makes recruit claustrophobic.	Claustrophobia makes recruit rave.	Paul and Kat slap recruit to keep him from running.

What do you think would have happened if Paul and Kat had ignored his raving? Why do you think some soldiers suffer mental collapse during battle and others do not?

6. What does Paul mean, "We do not fight, we defend ourselves against annihilation" (page 113)? (The men are not fighting for a cause; they are instinctively striking out for survival.) Does he regret killing men like the one with the pointed beard? (At the time, he kills madly, without much reflection.)

7. As horrible as warfare is, and as exhausted as Paul and the others are, why don't they just drop and lie where they fall? (They are angry, conditioned to fight, and know they have to do their part, as their friends are doing.)

8. Which soldiers are being fed better—the Germans or their enemies? What does this say about the Germans' prospects for winning the war? [Their enemies have better food, more supplies; the Germans are weakening. Historically (such as in he U. S. Civil War) troops with better provisions are the more successful.]

9. What memories from childhood sweep over Paul? (He suddenly remembers a summer evening in the cathedral garden; sitting by the poplars that line a stream, as a boy.) Why do you suppose these memories are always so "quiet" and calm? Why is quietness unattainable at the front (page 121)? What is the significance of the contrast between that observation and the title phrase?

10. Why do the soldiers hunt for copper driving-bands and silk parachutes? (souvenirs; presents for women) Does this remind you of anything from more recent wars (such as the Gulf War)?

11. What happens when Himmelstoss panics and refuses to fight? (Paul orders him to fight but Himmelstoss remains frozen.) Why is the lieutenant successful in galvanizing him where Paul is not? (Himmelstoss responds to the order from a superior since he is conditioned to do so.)

12. How do you feel at the end of this chapter? horrified? disgusted? numb? Did you feel that you were "there" on the battlefield—or that you had been kept at a distance from the action?

    PREDICTION: What will it be like for Paul when he goes home on leave?

Writing Idea
Pretend that you are writing a short chapter for a history textbook. Write an objective description of the action in this chapter. Before you write the first draft, discuss what parts you will leave out and how you must change the language.

Literary Analysis: Contrast
Contrast is a striking difference between two things. An author may use contrasting images or ideas to clarify a situation. What is the contrast between this chapter and the previous one? How is the action—and the atmosphere—different? (Chapter 5 is relatively relaxed and peaceful whereas Chapter 6 is full of the horrors of war.) Have students look for contrasting chapters throughout the book.

Chapter 7

Vocabulary

foraging 138	ornamental 139	quixotic 139	smutty 143
billeted 143	crafty 144	tunic 149	brothels 150
silhouette 154	precipitously 155	mottled 156	stagnant 156
confectioner's 157	apoplexy 161	stupefied 163	skittle 164
uproariously 166	johnnies 167	sectors 168	compensation 175
skirmishing 176	contemptuously 179	disperses 180	destitute 184

Discussion Questions

1. How do things improve for Paul and the other survivors? (They are off duty for a while.) Are you surprised that they can seem so relaxed and good-humored so soon after seeing so much death and destruction?

2. What does Paul mean, "...after the war...shall begin the disentanglement of life and death"? (There will be continuing psychic damage to the soldiers.) Is this like the post-traumatic stress suffered by so many Vietnam veterans?

© Novel Units, Inc. All rights reserved

3. How does the poster make Paul and Albert feel? (They like looking at the pretty woman, remembering what peacetime was like.) Contrast their reaction with Leer's and Tjaden's. (The latter two make foul comments.) Why do Paul and Albert go off to the delousing station? (This makes them feel more "human"—worthy of such a girl.)

4. Why don't the women come down and have a picnic with Paul and the others when they first meet? (Both are forbidden to cross the canal.) Why do you think they are interested in each other? (In addition to mutual physical attraction, the women are hungry and see the prospect of food.)

5. Why do Paul, Kropp, and Leer give Tjaden so much rum? (They want him to sleep through the rendezvous, as there are only three women for four men.)

6. Why is Paul reluctant to go on leave? (Life is good where he is, for the moment; he worries about whether he will meet up with his friends again when he returns.) How does the French woman react to the news? (She doesn't take much notice, since he is not going into battle.) How do they feel about the fact that they will never see each other again? (Paul is irritated that it doesn't seem to bother the woman.)

7. What do you "see" as Paul reunites with his family? What do you think would have made the reunion a happier one for him?

8. What sorts of conflict does Paul undergo while on leave? (Man against Man and Inner Conflict) Why does he get angry with the major? (The major "pulls rank" and faults him for accidentally failing to salute.) How does he feel himself distanced from his father? (His father wants to show off his son in uniform.) Why can't he talk to his mother about how he really feels? (He feels that he must be the strong one and does not want to let her know the horrors he faces.) Why doesn't he enjoy being at the table with his German-master and the other teachers? (They continue to talk about the glory of war.)

9. How do you imagine Paul's room? What is it that used to make him feel a "powerful, nameless urge"—but does so no longer (page 171)? (reading) Why doesn't he feel at home here anymore? (His reality is on the battlefield.)

10. Who is Mittelstaedt? (a classmate of Paul's who has become a commander) How does he get revenge on Kantorek? (As Kantorek's commander, he humiliates Kantorek in much the same way the teacher used to humiliate him.) Do you think Kantorek's views on war have changed? Does this remind you of another part of this story? (getting even with Himmelstoss)

11. Does Paul find it hard to talk to Kemmerich's mother? (yes) Why doesn't he tell her the truth? (He doesn't want her to know that her son suffered before he died.) Should he? What would you do in Paul's place?

12. What do you think would happen if Paul wept and told his mother how he really feels? Why do you suppose he doesn't consider staying home—deserting? Why do you think he feels that he shouldn't have come home?

PREDICTION: When Paul gets to see some of his enemies close up in a Russian prison camp, what will he think of them?

Writing Ideas
a) Describe Paul's room as you imagine it.
b) Write the speech that Paul might give his teacher's class.

Literary Analysis: Irony
An ironic situation is one in which there is a contrast between appearance and reality. What is ironic about the fact that Paul's mother tells him to watch out for loose women and be careful at the front? (She has no idea of the reality of the situation: There are few women and there is no way to be careful; war is horrible and Paul faces death every moment.)

Chapters 8-9

Vocabulary

opalescent 188	dysentery 190	grovelling 191	intrigues 193
peevish 202	interject 203	obtuse 204	extenuation 211
abstraction 223	irresolutely 224	stratagem 225	

Discussion Questions

1. How does Paul spend his time at the training camp? (training during the day, playing the piano at the Soldier's home in the evenings; visiting sometimes with his sister and father.) Is he lonely? How can you tell that he enjoys Nature? (He describes the beauty of the sand and the woods—page 188.)

2. How does Paul feel when he sees the enemy—Russian soldiers—close up? (He is surprised that they look as kindly as any German peasants.) When he sees them going through the garbage, is he disgusted? (somewhat, but more distressed) When he sees how hungry they are, does he feel sorry for them? (yes) Is he curious about them? (yes) How are they like Germans? How are they different? (As a whole-class activity, use a diagram on the chalkboard like the one on page 19 to compare the two groups.)

Russian Soldiers	Germans
honest faces	honest faces
good boots	bad boots
poor or no provisions	mediocre provisions
frequent deaths	frequent deaths
war over for them	must keep fighting

3. What is Paul's attitude toward war, now? What does he mean, "A word of command has made these silent figures our enemies; a word of command might transform them into our friends." (page 193)? (In peacetime, they would probably be friends of his.)

4. Looking to the future, how does Paul plan to live again "after this annihilation of all human feeling" (page 194)? What will he do to give meaning to the meaningless slaughter in which he was engaged? (He will stifle his anti-war impulses now, but spread the word after the war is over.) How does this resolution parallel Remarque's actual post-war life? (Remarque wrote several novels illustrating the horrors of war after serving himself and being wounded five times.)

5. What music do you "hear" in this chapter? (the prisoner playing folk songs on his violin; the Russians singing at the burial) How does the music enhance the mood of the story?

6. Why do you think the author includes the detail about Paul's mother's illness? What comment is he making about inequities in the German health care system? (Paul's mother is in a third-rate hospital, because care is so expensive.)

7. How does Paul feel about being reunited with what is left of his company? (ecstatic) Why does he eat the moldy potato cakes? (He wants his friends to have the better ones—he has been on leave, and they have not.)

8. How do the soldiers feel about preparing for the Kaiser's visit? (They are touchy about having to spiff up.) Are they impressed by him? (No; he is smaller and less powerful than they imagined.) What does Tjaden mean, "Hindenburg too, he has to stand up stiff to him, eh?" (page 202)? (Tjaden is referring to the German general and president who conducted the war effort from 1916 on.) Do they blame the Kaiser for their misery in war? (Paul points out that the Kaiser was against the war.)

9. Where do you see in this chapter, once again, expression of the idea that one group starts a war, but another group fights it? (Kat observes that emperors "require" a war to gain notoriety.) Kropp wonders if there could have been a war if the Kaiser and 20 or 30 people in the world had said "No." Who determines in today's world whether there will be a war? Who fights the wars?

10. According to the soldiers' conclusions, who profits from war? (the leaders such as emperors and generals who become famous) Consider some recent wars in which Americans have become involved. Who has profited? Do you see any parallels between the characters' observations and your own?

11. What sort of propaganda does Paul resent? (lies about the Germans, such as statements that they eat Belgian children) Did Germany use propaganda against its enemies during WWI? Do we use propaganda during wartime, today? (Propaganda is always a factor in war—the enemy must be made to seem inhuman in order to engender support for the war.)

12. Compare and contrast Paul and the Frenchman. How are the men similar? How are they different?

Paul	Frenchman
seeks refuge in shellhole	seeks refuge in shellhole
has parents and sister	has wife and daughter
wants to live	wants to live

What do you "see" as Paul attacks the Frenchman and waits for him to die? What is Paul going through? How do you feel toward each man? Are you surprised that Paul later tells Kat and Albert about the killing? They try to comfort him by saying, "What else could you have done?" Did he have other choices? Would he do the same thing again?

PREDICTION: Will Paul notify the family of Gerard Duval?

Writing Idea
Paul is startled to realize that the "enemy"—the Russian soldiers—are men very like himself. Describe a time when you had a similar experience—you realized that someone or some group of people is not as different from you as you had imagined.

Literary Analysis: Point of View
There are two basic ways an author may present the events in the story: first person narrator ("I") or third person narrator ("he"). From whose point of view is the story told? (Paul's) What are the advantages and disadvantages of using this point of view? (The reader has a sense of immediacy—of listening to the speaker as he tells his story; the reader is privy only to Paul's thoughts, observations, perceptions.)

Chapter 10

Vocabulary

punctually 236	griping 237	fastidious 238	baldaquin 239
evacuate 239	perambulators 239	evade 248	tuition 249
quicksilver 250	commissariat 252	mortuary 258	abyss 263
mantilla 266	napkin 266		

Discussion Questions

1. Why do Paul and the others consider guarding the village a "good job" (page 231)? (They have access to plenty of food and supplies.) Do you find any humor—however macabre—in this section? (They make their feast in the middle of a shelling.)

2. Why does Paul feel that "the war is too desperate to allow us to be sentimental for long...we cannot afford to be anything but matter-of-fact"? (If they acknowledged their fear, they would "crack.") Wouldn't it be better if the soldiers could express how they feel? Have you ever been in a situation where you had to hold back your feelings?

3. Reread the passage where Albert and Paul pack the bed onto the lorry (page 238). How would you illustrate the truck as it carries the soldiers away from the village? What expressions would you put on the men's faces?

4. Are you surprised when Paul and Albert are hit? Why does Paul decide not to make a sound as the doctor tends his wounds? (He fears being chloroformed and waking up missing a limb.)

5. How does Paul arrange to stay with Albert? (He heats the thermometer to make it appear that they both have fevers and are both sent to the same hospital.)

6. What does Remarque's attitude toward doctors seem to be? (He points out that though there are good ones, some are cruel—causing unnecessary pain, experimenting on human guinea pigs—and others are callous.) Do you think the German doctors were really as callous and sadistic as he portrays them?

7. How is Paul embarrassed by the young sister? (He is ashamed to tell her he has lice, needs a bedpan.) Are you surprised that he is so easily shamed after all that he has seen on the battlefield?

8. Why do the soldiers yell at the sisters? (They want the door closed so they aren't disturbed by the sisters' praying.) Do you think they are being ungrateful?

9. What does Paul mean, "With Josef Hamacher in our midst we can now risk anything" (page 254)? (Hamacher has been wounded in the head and is therefore not held accountable for his actions. He can take the blame for anything they do.)

10. The hospital scene is almost light in tone up to a certain point. Where does that change? (Franz Wächter hemorrhages and dies.) Where do horrifying details begin to accumulate? (pages 256-257, with the introduction of the "Dying Room") How does the scene with Lewandowski and his wife provide some relief from the horror? (In a comical, touching scene, the men look the other way and entertain the baby while Lewandowski and his wife make love.)

11. Are you surprised by what happens to Peter? (He returns from the Dying Room; most probably had predicted that he would die.) Why do you suppose the author provided this outcome? Wouldn't it have been more realistic and consistent to have him die like all the others who were sent to the "Dying Room"? (It shows that mental determination can overcome seemingly impossible odds—something that really does happen from time to time.)

12. Why is Albert so depressed? (His leg has been amputated.) Why doesn't he commit suicide? (He has the support of his friends.) Would most people rather be dead than lose a limb?

PREDICTION: What will happen to the narrator when the war ends?

Writing Idea
Describe the dream that Paul has one night while recovering in the hospital.

Literary Analysis: Satire
Satire is the use of ridicule, sarcasm, wit, or irony to expose a folly or social evil. Reread the section where Paul describes the operations for flat feet (pages 259-260). What aspect of the medical profession is Remarque condemning? (The surgeons' unethical use of soldiers as guinea pigs causes the soldiers to be in worse shape than before the surgery.)

Chapters 11-12

Vocabulary

solidarity 272	banal 272	differentiated 273	regeneration 274
degeneration 274	aberration 277	obliquely 278	simulated 279
niggardliness 285	armistice 285	insensate 285	mystified 291
superfluous 294	divinations 295	rowan 295	

Discussion Questions

1. What does Paul mean, "It is as though formerly we were coins of different provinces; and now we are melted down, and all bear the same stamp" (page 272)? (When men fight side by side in war, distinctions based on birth, education, etc. no longer matter.)

2. Why does Detering desert? Why does the cherry tree have such an impact on him? (The blossoms remind him of springtime at home and he longs to return there.) Are you surprised that more men haven't deserted up until now? What do you suppose happens to him? (He is captured by the military police and perhaps executed.)

3. How can you tell that the Germans are losing the war? (They are sending in more and more young recruits; supplies and food are low.) How does Paul feel about that? (He just wants it all to be over.)

4. How do the soldiers comfort themselves, keep themselves from going crazy? (They turn into unthinking animals; rely on comradeship; live for the moment.)

5. Why does Paul tell about how Berger gets injured? (to show that soldiers are being uncharacteristically careless; Berger goes after a messenger dog.) What does this show about the morale of the troops? (It is low.)

6. "Müller is dead." (page 279) Why do you think Paul describes the death of his friend so succinctly, so matter-of-factly? What does this show about his emotions? (He is numb.) How does he seem to feel now, compared with his attitude at the beginning of the book? (hopeless, dazed, withdrawn)

7. What has happened to Kemmerich's boots? (After Müller died, they passed on to Paul.) How can you tell that Paul has admitted to himself that he may well die? (He has promised them to Tjaden.)

8. Where do you see again in this section the ironic contrast between those who profit from war and those who fight it? (page 280: "The factory owners in Germany have grown wealthy...")

9. Where do you see Remarque's dislike of military doctors coming up again in this chapter? (Paul mentions the doctors who are eager to return the injured to battle.) Explain Kat's joke about the staff surgeon (page 281). (Kat is implying that staff surgeons have "wooden heads"—are stupid and unfeeling.)

10. What do you see, hear, smell, feel as Bertinck and Leer are hit?

11. How does Paul contrast his observations of Nature and the war in the Summer of 1918? (The days are beautiful—"blue and gold," the poppies bloom, the evenings are warm—and the war is bloody.) What is his state of mind? (bleak, bitter, horrified, frustrated, despairing that he may die before the war ends)

12. How does Kat die? (Kat is wounded and Paul puts him on his shoulders; a splinter hits Kat in the head and kills him.) Why do you think Remarque has Kat be the last friend of Paul's to go? How do the words, "All is usual" belie Paul's feelings?

13. How does Paul feel now that he believes that the war is ending? (numb, helpless, hopeless) What does he mean, "All that meets me…are but feelings…but no aims" (page 294)? (His future is bleak, his ambitions crushed.) Do you see any similarities between his concerns—and the problems that post-war veterans of Vietnam faced?

14. Why do you think Remarque has Paul die at the end? Why do you think he has the death come on a quiet day? Why would his expression indicate he was glad to die? How does his death lend meaning to the title? (Paul finally has the quiet and peace he dreamed of so often.)

Writing Idea
You are Paul. Kat has just died and a flood of memories rises to the surface of your mind. Describe the memories. You may choose to use the stream-of-consciousness technique—reproducing the uninterrupted flow of thoughts, feelings, associations, and memories that take place in Paul's mind, without worrying about complete sentences. Or you might like to try capturing the memories in a poem.

Literary Analysis: Symbol
A *symbol* is a person, place, event, or object that suggests something further. For example, the dove is a symbol of peace. In literature, objects may be used to represent abstract ideas. Repeated appearances of a particular object throughout a story may signal that the object is being used as a symbol. Where do you see the boots mentioned in the story? (repeatedly, from the time when Kemmerich gives them up to Müeller to near the end of the story, when Paul says he will give them to Tjaden) What might they symbolize? (the inability to escape death; these symbols of mortality are passed from one soldier to the next until the entire company is dead)

Post-Reading Extension Activities

Questions for Discussion or Writing

1. How did the ending make you feel? Were you surprised? How did the point of view change—and why?
2. In what ways are the issues in this book specific to World War I? In what ways does this book apply to war in general? What changes would have to be made if the narrator were a French or American soldier? What aspects of the story would remain the same?
3. As you replay this novel in your mind, which images stand out? Which parts do you find most horrifying? Did you laugh at anything? Where was the tension highest for you? Do you have any unanswered questions about the novel?
4. Do you feel that Paul changes during the course of the novel? What, if anything, does he learn?
5. Reread the preface to the novel. Has Remarque accomplished what he set out to do? What would you say to those who claim that the book is an accusation—that it is a criticism of the German war machine? What would you say to those who claim that the book is an adventure—that it is a piece of romantic propaganda for war?
6. *All Quiet on the Western Front* contains many accounts of soldiers driven to exhaustion, given inadequate medical care, sent into situations where they were almost certain to be killed. Why did the soldiers tolerate these conditions? Why didn't more of them revolt or run away?
7. Discuss how the following themes are developed in *All Quiet on the Western Front*:
    - courage and fear
    - empathy and self-preservation
    - hope and despair
8. How is Nature—particularly animals—described throughout the novel? What is Remarque saying about Nature and human nature?
9. What do you get from this story that you would not get from a nonfiction text about World War I? What would you get from the text that you do not get from the novel?
10. What are the advantages and disadvantages of having Paul narrate the story?
11. *All Quiet on the Western Front* is considered a "classic." Why do you think it has endured so long? What makes it "great"? (Brainstorm a list of criteria with classmates.)
12. How would you describe Paul's tone throughout the story? Is he bitter? Would you expect him to be? Does his tone change?

Suggested Further Reading
1. Other historical fiction about war:

    Across Five Aprils (Irene Hunt)
    The Last Mission (Harry Mazer)
    No Hero for the Kaiser (Rudolf Frank)
    The Red Badge of Courage (Stephen Crane)
    Bridge of San Luis Rey (Wilder)
    A Farewell to Arms (Hemingway)
    War and Peace (Tolstoy)
    The Naked and the Dead (Mailer)
    Catch 22 (Heller)
    Slaughterhouse Five (Vonnegut)

2. Other books by Remarque:

    The Road Back, Three Comrades, Flotsam, Arch of Triumph, Spark of Life, A Time to Love and a Time to Die, The Black Obelisk, Heaven Has No Favorites, Night in Lisbon

Writing
1. Choose another novel about war (such as *The Red Badge of Courage;* see the list above). Explore how this book's characters, tone, themes, and point of view parallel or contrast with those in *All Quiet on the Western Front.*
2. Essay topic: Below is a quote by Herbert Hoover

    "Older men declare war. But it is youth who must fight and die. And it is youth who must inherit the tribulation, the sorrow, and the triumphs that are the aftermath of war."
    Herbert Hoover—June 27, 1944

    Elaborate on how Remarque develops this idea in *All Quiet on the Western Front.*
3. Essay topic: Analyze how Remarque uses the device of contrast to develop ideas and enhance the emotional impact on the reader.
4. Trace and analyze the appearance of Kemmerich's boots throughout the novel.
5. Explain the significance of the title.
6. Pretend that you are Paul and that you keep a journal. Write five or six entries from the period described in the novel.
7. Assume the persona of Paul or one of the other characters in the novel. Write a letter home.
8. Write the prayer that one of the characters in the novel might utter (silently or aloud).

9. Respond to an episode in the story with a poem. It might be a poem of confession, bitterness, thanks, a once-then approach, or another form you choose.

10. Write a newspaper article about an incident related to the story (such as the obituary that might appear in Paul's hometown paper after his death).

11. Write a poem that captures Paul's feelings about how the older generation sends young men off to war. You might create the poem around one line of the story, elaborating on the two contrasting ideas found there.

    For example, page 13:

    "While they continued to write and talk...

    _____

    ...we saw the wounded and dying."

    _____

12. Choose a section of the story where you find the language to be particularly striking and recast that section as a poem by eliminating unnecessary words, inserting line breaks, and adding lines of your choice. (For example, you might start with the passage on the top of page 283: "Shells, gas clouds, and flotillas of tanks...trenches, hospitals, the common grave...")

13. Read the poem, "War is Kind," by Stephen Crane. Analyze the poem and compare it with Remarque's novel. How are the themes and language similar? Try rewriting Crane's poem to include some details from the novel.

Listening/Speaking

1. **Interview:** Several students assume the roles of key characters (such as Paul, Kat, Himmelstoss and Albert). The rest of the students prepare questions for members of the panel, who answer in character. (e.g., "Kat—Do you think your age has made it easier or harder for you to cope with being on the battlefield?")

2. **Debate:** Hold a classroom debate on the following statements. (Students who agree get on one side of the room. Students who disagree get on the other. Those with no opinion stay in the middle. Both sides try to convince the students who remain in the middle.)
   - Suffering builds a man's character.
   - War is seldom necessary.

Drama
1. Rewrite a scene from the novel in play form, then act it out (e.g., the scene where Paul stabs the French soldier, then tends his wound).
2. Act out a scene that is not shown in the novel. For instance, how do Paul and his friends celebrate Paul's birthday? What would Paul's homecoming have been like, had he lived?

Art
1. Choose a scene from the story—such as the one where Paul and the others prepare a feast in the midst of a shelling attack—and create a group mural that will interest other students in reading the novel.
2. Choose a scene in which you find a powerful description—such as the description of the dying horses—and illustrate it with markers or watercolors.

Music
1. Find examples of music that Paul and other young people of that time might have enjoyed. Were there any songs about World War I?
2. Many songs have been written about war. Share some of these recordings and discuss which ones convey the feelings Paul and the others have about the battlefield.

Research
1. Create a colorful timeline to show events that served as a backdrop to the story, such as the assassination of Archduke Ferdinand in June 1914 and the German invasion of France in August 1914. Include events from the story on your timeline.
2. The Kaiser appears in the story. Find out more about the real-life Kaiser.
3. Find out more about the trench warfare of World War I. How accurately does the novel depict it?
4. Identify some of the problems that Germany faced after the war. Which of these were suggested in *All Quiet on the Western Front*?
5. Find out more about the diagnosis, "post traumatic stress disorder." With what emotional problems would Paul and his friends have had to cope if they had survived the war? How does a therapist today treat individuals with that disorder?